Milly, M... and the Jungle Gym

"We may look different but we feel the same."

Miss Blythe folded her arms. "If you want a jungle gym," she said, "you'll have to raise the money yourselves."

Milly, Molly and their friends put their heads together and came up with a plan. A Business Plan.

Miss Blythe was amazed.
"A cookie factory!" she exclaimed.

Alf was the maths whiz. He prepared the budget and the quantities.

Sophie was the methodical one.
She made a list of ingredients and Poppy
helped her buy them.

Milly and Molly were practised mixers.
They mixed and mixed.

Jack was good with the oven.
He baked the cookies golden brown.

Meg was the meticulous one.
She did the icing.

Tom had an eye for the middle. He placed the jellybeans.

And Humphrey – well, he took care of quality control!

Elizabeth had the neatest writing. She did the packaging and labelling.

George's negotiating skills were sharp.
His department was sales.

Miss Blythe provided transport and Harry was the banker.

By the end of the month there was one bag of cookies left and...

... Harry's bank bag was bulging.

"There's enough money here to buy a jungle gym," said the shopkeeper.
"It will be delivered tomorrow," he promised.

And it was.

"I'm very proud of you all," said Miss Blythe.
"You have shown great cooperation and teamwork…"

Miss Blythe was interrupted by a group of agitated gentlemen.
"We've sold out of cookies," they shouted.
"When is your next delivery?"

Before Miss Blythe could say a word,

Milly, Molly and their friends had raced off.

"This is a school, not a cookie factory,"
Miss Blythe said bluntly.

The agitated gentlemen strode off and Miss Blythe collapsed with the very last bag of cookies. She was exhausted.

But Milly, Molly and their friends were no such thing. They had worked very hard for their jungle gym. Now it was time to play.